J

Mills, Ron

Kingdom tales

KINGDOM TALES

FIVE STORIES JESUS TOLD

Ron Mills

Abingdon Press
Nashville

KINGDOM TALES

This book is printed on recycled, acid-free paper.

ISBN 0-687-089611

Cover illustrated by Bob Pepper. Text illustrated by Nell Fisher.

98 99 01 02 03 04 05 06 07—10 9 8 7 6 5 4 3 2 1

MANUFACTURED IN THE UNITED STATE OF AMERICA

CONTENTS

Kingdom Tales: Five Stories Jesus Told

SOWING LESSONS

I climbed the familiar tree beside the road. My father slung the seed bag over his shoulder and stepped out into the field. He swept his arm in a familiar arc, rhythmically scattering grain on the plowed ground. I watched him sow the seed. Out of the corner of my eye, I detected movement. The dust cloud in the distance escorted a band of people toward us. They grew closer. I could see the group centered around one man. He was talking as they reached the shade of my tree.

"Look at this farmer," the man said to the group, as he pointed to my father working in the field.

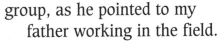

They seemed eager to hear his words. "See him scatter grain seed. Some of the seed has fallen on the path here. We have trampled on it. Look, the birds have discovered the seed and already are feeding on it."

The people kept their attention on the man. They listened to every word. He walked near the rocky border of my father's field.

"Seed has fallen here too," the man continued. "It may sprout. There is not enough soil to hold the moisture the seed needs to survive. The seed will dry out."

Kingdom Tales: Five Stories Jesus Told

I had been watching the group sitting on the ground beneath me. I did not notice the silence until someone below me looked up into the tree. I glanced at the teacher. He looked straight at me.

"A tree is a great place to listen to stories isn't it?" he asked me. I nodded my head nervously. "What is your name, boy?" he asked.

"Timeon," I replied.

"Is your father the farmer?" he asked.

"Yes," I answered.

"I helped my father when I was a boy too," he said.

The man smiled then looked back at his listeners. He walked to where the thistles and weeds grew near the edge of the field.

"No doubt some seed has fallen among these thorns. It will begin to grow. But not for long. Thorns will choke the young plants."

Then the teacher walked out into my father's field. He scooped up a handful of rich soil.

"Ahh, the seed falling on the soil Timeon's father has worked will do more than sprout. It will grow and produce much grain."

He moved toward the crowd, waved his hand as if to dismiss them. He said, "Let those who have ears to hear, hear."

He stopped talking, walked to the tree, and sank back against its trunk. Some of the people stood and dusted themselves off. They began to make their way slowly down the road. They talked among themselves as they traveled.

Another group of men, though, stayed near the teacher beneath the tree.

"This story, Rabbi," one of the men said with his voice full of questions, "what does it mean?"

"Your heart, Nathaniel," the teacher answered, "the heart of all human beings, is like soil. One

Kingdom Tales: Five Stories Jesus Told

day God's word falls into the heart. In some persons it lies on the surface. They never understand its power nor really desire to. God's presence is passed by on the way to the rest of their lives. They trample it down like they would a seed sown on a path."

"I don't understand," the man named Nathaniel said, "why some do not believe in God?"

"A mysterious power keeps some from ever hearing God's voice," the teacher replied.

Nathaniel sat back, thinking.

"And the rocky soil?" another one around the tree asked.

"Some people listen to God's promises," the leader said. "They seem to believe. But their trust grows only as deep as their comfort. When life becomes difficult, they panic. They trust God less and less. Soon, any faith they had withers like a sprout in the summer's heat."

"What about the thorny soil, master?" another man asked.

"Many people listen to the way of God. The talk of faith interests them. But they spend so much energy trying to be rich and at ease. They worry about buying something else or taking care of what they already have. God never has a chance to change them. They never have time to think deeply about their lives. In the end, the way of God gets crowded out of their busy, fretful lives."

"What about my dad's good soil?" I blurted out from the branches of the tree without thinking.

"Oops, sorry," I said.

The teacher and the men all laughed loudly. "Well, Timeon," the teacher said, "some people do listen to God's word when it falls into their lives. They hold onto its promises. They trust in God through difficult places as well as comfortable places. God can work with their hearts and God changes them. They become persons who grow strong in faith. They help others believe in God by their good life. Which soil do you want to be Timeon?" the teacher asked me.

"I want to be way out there in the good soil my dad is planting now."

They all laughed again.

"Somehow Timeon," the teacher answered, "God knows your heart. Listen for God's voice."

He stood up and dusted himself off. The men did the same. He reached up toward me. I extended my hand to him. He grasped my hand in his.

"Thank you for the shade of a very friendly tree," he said smiling up at me. "God's seed is falling in your life even now Timeon. Listen for God's words. You will hear them in your heart. Follow the Father's voice and you will find life."

"Good-bye," I shouted from the tree branches as they walked away. They all waved.

In the distance my father finished the last section of the field. He turned and walked back toward the tree. I swung down from the branch, landing on the ground.

"Who were all those people?" my father asked.

"I don't know any of them," I said. "They were all listening to one man talk about God though."

"About God?" my father said curiously. "Well, what did he say?"

"Well, he started by talking about you, really."

"About me?"

"Yes, about you, and the places you have scattered your grain seed."

My father and I walked toward home talking. I glanced behind us at the storytelling tree. It grew smaller in the distance. The teacher was right: it was a great place to listen to stories. I would never forget the one I heard today.

Kingdom Tales: Five Stories Jesus Told

THE
BUILDING
PROJECT

"It is such a pretty day Grandfather," I said with a question in my voice.

"I can tell by the way you are talking," my grandfather replied, "you are not just talking about a beautiful day."

Grandfathers are wise. "Well," I began slowly, "it is such a clear day. It has been rainy all week. Going to church . . . well . . . will take up the best part of the morning. Do you think . . . ."

"We can skip church today?" Grandfather interrupted.

"Umm . . . yea," I answered excitedly.

"Well if we do," Grandfather continued, "I might miss the next step in my building project."

"What?" I asked. "What building project? Are they working on something at the church?"

"I know what we can do, Jammy," my grandfather called me that because the initials of my name, Justin Avery Miller, spelled the word J.A.M., "we will take a different way to church today. Near the church there is an interesting thing to see."

After Grandfather and I finished breakfast, we quickly dressed. Grandfather explained to my grandmother we would be leaving for church a little earlier than usual.

"I will get a ride from Eunice," she said. "No need for you to worry about me."

I bounced down the porch steps. I ran across the yard to the old white station wagon parked under the open shed. My excitement grew as grandfather backed out of the driveway and headed toward this mysterious place. I could not imagine what it might be.

Kingdom Tales: Five Stories Jesus Told

After driving awhile, Grandfather turned onto a narrow road. We wound our way through the woods a short distance. He brought the station wagon to a stop in front of a large brick home. It looked like a new home but it was abandoned. The grass had grown into choking weeds. The shrubbery around the house was wildly overgrown. It covered the windows and hung over the front porch.

"No one lives here, Grandfather," I said, wide-eyed.

"Not anymore," he replied. "Let's step back and look for a second."

We walked over and stood directly in front of the house.

"Tell me," Grandfather said, "can you see anything that might have made this house unlivable?"

I looked and looked. "No sir," I said.

"Several years ago a man moved into our area. He picked out this lot, because it has such a pretty view of Shepherd's Valley. The soil here is made up of a high concentration of sandy loam. The neighbors told the man that, although the view was beautiful, it was not a good place to build a house. The carpenters and the brickmasons warned him too. But the man insisted he knew what was best. He wanted his house built here no matter what. So the man built his house on this spot despite all the warnings.

"It was a lovely home when he finished it. Soft green grass covered the yard. Beautiful landscaping surrounded the house. The best view in the whole county unfolded before it. A couple of years ago though, rain fell steadily on Shepherd's Valley. The ground stayed soaked for weeks. Shepherd's Creek over there," Grandfather pointed behind the house, "flowed out of its banks into the yard. Not long after the flood the man called the carpenters back.

Some cracks in the ceiling of his kitchen needed repairing. They told him then that the house was settling. It would crack some more."

"Follow me around here," my grandfather said. We walked around the house to the back. The rear corner of the house had sunk down into the ground. The roof had collapsed. Bricks had fallen to the ground exposing the inside of the house.

"The house did keep cracking and settling. The man tried everything to save it. But there was nothing he could do. With each soaking rain the house sank into the soil. Finally, the man and his family could only abandon it. They left broken hearted. It was a tremendous loss."

Kingdom Tales: Five Stories Jesus Told

The Building Project

"Why didn't the man listen to those who tried to warn him?" I asked.

"Sometimes," my grandfather said, "there are places that seem so beautiful, we do not notice their danger. We think we know best. We end up not listening to those who try to warn us. We have enough money or enough strength to do whatever we want. We do something because we can. Later, we know the sadness."

"I showed you this house," my grandfather told me, "because when your grandmother and I first came to Shepherd's Valley, we wanted to build our home right over there." He pointed to a place near the abandoned house. "The builders told us about the sand and the loam. We were disappointed because this is such a beautiful place with a lovely view. But we listened to the builders. We built in a place where we discovered bedrock. The rock provided a firm foundation for the house. Our house has stood for fifty years. We raised our family there. Many times through the years we have been thankful for the shelter it has provided. Let's get back in the car," Grandfather said, "Church services will begin soon."

We started back down the drive and headed for church. My grandfather began speaking again, "I told you earlier this morning I go to church because it helps me with my building project. I learned to think of my life as a building project from the Bible. Jesus said to a group of people, 'Everyone who

The Building Project

hears these words of mine and listens is like a person who built a house on a rock. The rains fell, and the floods came. The winds blew and beat on that house. It did not fall, because it had been built on the rock. And everyone who hears these words of mine and does not do them will be like a foolish person who built a house on the sand. The rains fell, and the floods came. The winds blew and beat against that house. It fell.'

"One day you will discover where you build your house is important. Where you build your heart is important too. Many places will look beautiful to

Kingdom Tales: Five Stories Jesus Told

you. You will want to build your life on them. Some of those places are not trustworthy. They will end up letting your heart sink and collapse. Jammy, when God sent Jesus to us, God sent a wise, master builder of the heart. Jesus leads us to places we can trust with our lives. So we could have skipped church today and enjoyed this sunny weather. But I'm working on building this house called my life. Jesus' words help me. I hope you listen for his words to you today. Believe me. You can trust them. Jesus will help you build everything wisely."

The Building Project

Kingdom Tales: Five Stories Jesus Told

THE HORIZON

Many months have passed since I said good-bye to my youngest son. I should not have been surprised at the way things turned out. Questions were always on his lips. His curiosity about the world never stopped. Through his childhood and his youth, he explored these meadows and hills with endless fascination.

"What lies at the end of the road, Father?" he asked me once about the road that wound its way past our house and disappeared in the horizon.

In my heart I knew a day would arrive when he would answer the question for himself. How it hurt to say good-

bye to him. In the end I could only give him my blessings and his due. I looked a long time into his face. I did not know if I would see those dreamer's eyes again. Though I was concerned, I gave him the money that was rightfully his.

His brother, ah, his brother is the stable one. He seems to have seen clearly and early on his place in life. Never has he gazed beyond our lands or longed to be somewhere else. He has been my right hand in overseeing what God has given us. So responsible has he been that I am afraid he has never understood his young brother's restlessness.

"Do not give this dreamer the whole amount," he pleaded with me. "He will only waste it, Father, and have nothing."

Always an eye towards tomorrow's needs, my eldest has. He reminds me often how difficult it is without his brother's help.

Still, I find myself gazing at the same horizon into which my son disappeared. I remember fondly the rhythm of his walk. Where will he end up, this pilgrim son of mine? Is he still alive? I do not know. I only feel the sadness creeping into my heart as I stare too long at the horizon.

The Horizon

But work must be done. I cannot tarry. *God be with you my son, wherever you are this day.* Perhaps God will comfort my heart in time. I must leave the horizon now to the stray dog rummaging in the distance. If that is a stray dog. I do not see too clearly yet.

No, the figure is too large for dog. Someone walking? I can't make it out. Yes. Someone walking. A neighbor perhaps, coming to buy a goat. But there is something familiar about that walk; the swing of the arms, the bounce of the head.

Kingdom Tales: Five Stories Jesus Told

"God be praised! Can it be?" I ask. It is! It is my boy! I must tell the servants to prepare a great feast! How weak he looks. How ragged his clothes are. My son who was lost to me is now found! This will be a day of celebration! He is alive and he is welcome no matter what he has done or what has happened to him!

Kingdom Tales: Five Stories Jesus Told

THE QUESTION

At the rear of a group of people, a lawyer sat. His arms were folded across his chest. He was listening to a man from Nazareth teaching. He listened for a few minutes, then stood and asked the teacher. "Jesus, I think that is your name," he said. "How can I be sure I will live with God always?" The lawyer looked around at the crowd. He looked back at Jesus, then he sat down.

Jesus stopped talking to the crowd. He turned his attention to the man who questioned him. "You are a lawyer, aren't you? What do you read in God's law?"

"People should love God with all of their heart and with all of their soul. They should love God with all of their strength and with all of their mind. They should love their neighbor as they love themselves." The lawyer sat down proudly. The people around him nodded their heads approvingly.

Jesus replied, "Good answer. If you do that, you will always live with God."

Jesus turned his attention back to the crowd,

intending to teach them. The lawyer grew somewhat agitated. He seemed to want something more than the answer Jesus gave him. Before Jesus spoke to the crowd again, the lawyer stood. He looked around the crowd to make sure they noticed him. "And just who is my neighbor?" he asked, with a smirk on his face.

Jesus waited for the lawyer to sit down. To everyone's surprise, he did not answer the lawyer's question but began to tell a story.

"A man was traveling one day between two towns," Jesus said. "He was attacked by some robbers who took all of his goods. They left him badly beaten on the side of the road. The man was unconscious. He looked dead.

In a little while a very religious man who led the services of worship walked down the road. He saw the man lying there. This religious leader crossed to the other side and passed by the wounded man."

"There's nothing wrong with that," the lawyer said to the people around him. "This man was a religious leader. Is it not written in the law that if a priest touches a dead body the priest becomes unable to lead services of worship? He cannot go to the Temple. This priest was right to walk on by. He may have thought the man was dead. He did nothing wrong."

Jesus heard the lawyer's response but said nothing. He continued the story he was telling. "A little while later another religious worker came walking down the road. Like the first person, this person too passed right by the wounded man."

"I do not think the second person did anything wrong either. Any respected religious leader must remain holy in order to serve God. If this person touched the traveler, he would not have been able to do religious work. That's what God's law says."

Again Jesus said nothing but continued telling the story. "Then a Samaritan traveled down the road," Jesus said.

"Now I don't understand this part," the lawyer said to those sitting nearby him. "Why is Jesus talking about a person with whom we have nothing to do? We avoid Samaritans don't we? We

Kingdom Tales: Five Stories Jesus Told

hate them. Why would any respectable teacher mention them? I just don't understand."

Jesus continued, "When this Samaritan saw the wounded man, he felt he wanted to help him. He went to him. He bandaged his wounds. He put the man upon his donkey, and carried him into the town. In the town the Samaritan found the wounded man a place to stay. He gave the innkeeper some money to take care of the man. He offered to pay anything extra when he returned."

Jesus looked at the lawyer. "Which of these three persons was a neighbor to the traveler who was beaten by the robbers?" he asked him. No one talked. Everyone turned to hear the lawyer's answer.

The lawyer muttered beneath his breath. "If he thinks I am even going to say the word 'Samaritan' he's wrong." The lawyer stood up and said "The one who showed love was a neighbor to the traveler."

"There," Jesus said, "you have answered your own questions. You can live with God always by loving God in every way you can and by loving your neighbor. A neighbor is not someone you choose. A neighbor is who you choose to be. Each of us can be a neighbor to people who need us in this moment. Go now and live like that. You will never have to worry about living with God when you choose to be a neighbor!"

The lawyer put his hand on his chin. Deep in

thought, he stood and walked away from the crowd. Jesus watched the lawyer depart, then turned his attention back to the crowd.

"Any more questions?" Jesus asked. No one said anything.

Kingdom Tales: Five Stories Jesus Told

THE SEED
IN THE MEADOW

One autumn a farmer called to his young daughter. "Allyson, take these seeds to the edge of the meadow and drop them there." Allyson delighted at the chance to visit the meadow again. It was such a beautiful place. She skipped all the way, holding tightly to the cloth bag holding the seeds.

When she reached the meadow's edge, Allyson carefully gathered the seeds from the bag. The seeds were so tiny. She sprinkled them in the air as she ran through the meadow.

One seed drifted gently down and landed

in a soft place at the edge of the green meadow. It lay on the ground beneath the grass of the field. Daily breezes pushed the loose soil against it. Every rainfall pounded its tiny hull into the soft earth. Days passed. The rain and wind buried the small seed under layers of dried grass, leaves, and soil. Soon the air grew crisp and cool. A snowflake landed nearby. Then another. The tiny seed lay covered beneath a fluffy blanket of snow.

One day, after months of wintry weather, the sun shown warm and bright. Something inside the tiny seed began to stir.

"Hmm . . . it's dark in here . . . and moist," the seed said. "Help! I'm trapped inside a circle. Anybody out there? Hold on, I think I've found some

Kingdom Tales: Five Stories Jesus Told

thing. Feels like a split in the side. Let's see. Maybe I can work myself through." The seed squirmed and wriggled.

"Whew! Almost through. A little more. There!

"Wait a minute! It's still dark in here. Hey! I'm surrounded by damp gritty stuff. Which way do I go? Up . . . down? Wait. I feel something. Something warm. Okay I'm headed that way. Here I go."

With a tremendous surge the seedling broke through the surface of the ground. "Yikes! It is so bright.

"Wow! Where am I? This place is full of huge things. I feel so small. How am I going to make it in a place like this?"

"A day at a time," a voice nearby said.

"Who said that?" the seedling asked.

"I did," said the fiddle-head fern, its green leafy stalks moving gently in the breeze. "Inside of you is a mystery waiting to come out. And it will in God's time."

"How? I'm so little," the seedling declared.

"Never confuse being little with being insignificant," the fern replied. "The life inside you is of God."

The Seed in the Meadow

"It is?" the seedling muttered.

"At times God surprises the world with unexpected outcomes. Little now does not necessarily mean little later."

As the days of spring grew warmer, the meadow changed rapidly. The seedling was so busy

Kingdom Tales: Five Stories Jesus Told

watching life in the meadow change it barely noticed the changes taking place in itself.

Spring turned into summer. Summer to fall. Soon the meadow lay blanketed with snow again. In God's time warm spring days returned and clothed the meadow with green. A lone robin flew with a strand of straw in its beak. It winged its way toward a familiar tree at the meadow's edge. The tree stood tall and green, stretching its branches out over a bed of ferns growing nearby. Sailing through the tree's crown, the robin landed gently in the fork of a branch. She tucked the straw into the tuft of twigs and grasses she had gathered on earlier flights. The robin left quickly to forage for more nest building materials.

"Whew!" the squeaky voice of a young sprout shouted down near the base of the tree in the meadow grass, "this place is huge. How will I make it here?"

"A day at a time," the wise green fern said.

"A day at a time," echoed the tall tree knowingly.

"Inside of you is a mystery waiting to come out. And it will," the fern said.

"A day at a time," the tree smiled.

"How do you know these things?" the squeaky young sprout asked.

As a solitary robin flew into its branches holding a strand of straw in its beak the tree said, "You'll see. You'll see."

Kingdom Tales: Five Stories Jesus Told